Stephanie Olds
The Leader Who Can't See Past Today

The Leader Who Can't See Past Today by Stephanie Olds

Copyright © 2025 by Ink and Revival Publishing

All rights reserved. This book or any portion thereof may not be reproduced or used in

any manner whatsoever without the express written permission of the publisher except for the use of brief quotations in a book review.

Printed in the United States of America December 2025

ISBN 978-1968178338

Ink and Revival Publishing Virginia, USA

Table of Contents

INTRODUCTION 1
1: The Myth of Busy Leadership 7
2: The Leader Who Can't See Past Today 15
3: The Cost of Reaction-Based Leadership 21
4: The Bottleneck Effect 29
5: The Psychology Behind Short-Sighted Leaders 37
6: Visionary Leadership—What It Actually Looks Like... 45
7: Leaders Who Build Systems Instead of Cycles 53
8: The Second-Order Consequence Mindset 61
9: Experiencing Different Leader Types 69
10: Becoming the Leader Your Workplace Deserves 77
11: When You're the Visionary in the Room 85
12: The Quiet Revolution of Forward-Thinking 93
CONCLUSION 99
Reflection Questions 103

Dedication

For the professionals who have carried clarity in rooms that could not see it.
For every forward thinker who trusted their vision even when the people around them could not understand it yet.

This book is for the ones who kept showing up with excellence, integrity, and foresight—
even when the environment made it difficult to breathe.

May you never again shrink your brilliance to match the limits of someone else's imagination.
May you rise into the leadership you were born for.
May your voice, your ideas, and your clarity stand without apology.

And to every person who has spent years navigating short-sighted leadership with grace:
I see you.
I honor you.
This book is yours.

Stephanie Olds

INTRODUCTION

When Leadership Has No Vision

"Where there is no vision, the people perish."

— Proverbs 29:18

There comes a point in every career where you can tell, almost instinctively, when the person guiding the work isn't actually guiding anything at all. They're moving, yes. They're responding. They're answering emails, scheduling meetings, and putting out whatever fire has managed to rise highest that day. But movement is not leadership, and noise is not direction, and urgency is not vision. It takes a long time to admit that truth out loud, especially when you've been taught to respect titles, honor hierarchy, and assume the person in charge must know something you don't. Yet over time, a different reality begins to reveal itself: some leaders are simply standing at the front, not leading from it.

You notice it first in the small things—the patterns that repeat because no one ever stopped long enough to ask why they keep happening. You see the way tasks replace strategy, and how every conversation circles the same drain of "what's due today" instead of "where are we trying to go." At first, you try to compensate quietly. You anticipate what they can't see, build what they don't plan for, and hold together the pieces they didn't realize were falling apart. It feels noble at the beginning. Necessary, even. But as the weeks become months, and the months become years, you begin to understand that you're not supporting a leader— you're carrying the consequences of their short-sightedness.

And that weight is subtle at first, almost invisible, until it isn't. Until it becomes the reason you stay up late trying to fix problems that didn't have to exist. Until it becomes the reason you walk into work already bracing for the next disruption you know is coming. Until it becomes the quiet exhaustion that settles into your bones, not because the work is hard, but because the leadership is small. Small in foresight, small in discipline, small in the imagination required to build something that lasts. That is when the truth begins to take shape: the leader who cannot see past today creates a workplace that never grows beyond survival.

Still, you try to understand them. You try to give grace, to believe they're doing the best they can with what they have. And sometimes they are. Sometimes they were promoted too quickly or trained too narrowly, rewarded for compliance instead of curiosity. Sometimes they simply mirror a system that has never asked anything more of them than to keep the machine running. But even when the reasons are understandable, the impact remains the same—teams become reactive, solutions become temporary, and the work becomes a never-ending loop of solving the same problem in slightly different ways.

The hardest part is recognizing what this dynamic does to people who are naturally forward-thinking. People who see patterns, anticipate outcomes, and instinctively build systems that prevent chaos instead of cleaning it up. To them, working under a leader without vision feels like living in a room with no windows. You can breathe, but not deeply. You can function, but not fully. You can contribute, but only in fragments, because everything in you that wants to build toward tomorrow is pulled back into the exhaustion of managing today. It is a slow suffocation of talent, creativity, and capacity—not because you lack capability, but because the environment refuses to rise to meet it.

And yet, this tension is not just a workplace inconvenience; it is a defining experience. It teaches you the difference between authority and leadership, between activity and progress, between being in charge and being transformational. It shows you what happens when vision is absent, and just as importantly, what becomes possible when vision finally appears. Every frustration becomes a case study. Every repeated problem becomes insight. Every moment you felt unseen becomes clarity about what true leadership must require. Over time, something quiet but powerful forms within you: a conviction that leadership is not about the next task, but the next horizon.

This book is born from that conviction. It is written for the people who have lived under short-sighted leadership and wondered if they were the problem. It is written for the ones who see what others miss, who think farther than they're allowed to plan, who carry the burden of future-thinking in workplaces that only live in the present. And it is written for the ones who want to lead differently—who want to build teams, structures, and systems that do more than survive the day.

Because the truth is simple: when leadership cannot see beyond today, neither can the work. But when leadership finally lifts its eyes toward what's coming, when it chooses foresight over reaction and design over chaos, everything changes. The work becomes intentional. The people become empowered. The vision becomes real. And the leader becomes worthy of the title.

"Activity is not leadership. Motion is not progress."

CHAPTER 1

The Myth of Busy Leadership

"What gets measured gets managed."

— *Peter Drucker*

There is a certain kind of leader who prides themselves on never stopping. They arrive early, leave late, and keep their calendars so full that there is barely room to breathe between obligations. They speak often about how much they're handling, how much is on their plate, how much pressure they're under. To the untrained eye, their pace looks impressive, even admirable. But the longer you watch, the more you notice something unsettling beneath the surface: all that movement isn't leading anywhere. They are busy, yes—but movement and progress are not the same, and the myth that they are is one of the quietest, most damaging illusions in leadership.

You begin to see the cracks when the same problems reappear week after week, untouched by anything resembling a lasting solution. Issues are addressed in fragments—just enough to survive the moment—before the leader rushes into the next meeting, the next email, the next performance of urgency. And because they never slow down long enough to think clearly, the fires they put out in the morning are already starting to smolder again by the afternoon. It becomes obvious that they are not moving with purpose; they are simply being carried by momentum, reacting to the day instead of directing it.

Still, people around them are conditioned to equate speed with competence. They assume a leader who is constantly in motion must be doing something meaningful. And this belief is reinforced every time the leader speaks of being overwhelmed, overworked, or stretched thin. Those admissions create a kind of unearned sympathy—a perception that they are sacrificing themselves for the good of the team. But sacrifice is not strategy, and exhaustion is not evidence of effectiveness. Sometimes it is simply evidence of disorganization, hidden behind the socially acceptable performance of being busy.

Over time, you begin to understand that busy leaders often rely on chaos as a kind of cover. When everything is urgent, nothing is questioned. When the pace is frantic, decisions are rarely examined. When the day feels out of control, no one has the space to notice that the leader is not leading—they are just struggling to keep up. And the faster they move, the more they avoid confronting the uncomfortable truth: that if they slowed down long enough to see the whole picture, they would have to acknowledge how much of the chaos is coming from them.

But the real cost of busy leadership is not borne by the leader. It is borne by the team. They are the ones who constantly adjust to shifting priorities, unclear instructions, and unfinished initiatives. They are the ones forced to fill in the gaps left by the leader's rush to the next task. They are the ones who quietly repair the consequences of decisions made without foresight. And they are the ones who eventually learn that no matter how hard they work, progress will always feel temporary in an environment where the leader never stops long enough to build anything sustainable.

> **"When urgency replaces clarity, teams learn**
> *to survive the day instead of shaping the future."*

What makes this dynamic even more exhausting is the subtle pressure it creates—an expectation that everyone else must also match the leader's frantic pace. Without ever saying it out loud, busy leaders build a culture where rest feels like laziness, reflection feels like delay, and thoughtful planning feels like a luxury no one can afford. The irony, of course, is that this is precisely why progress never takes root. Leadership that is always responding cannot design. Leadership that is always rushing cannot prioritize. Leadership that is always overwhelmed cannot elevate anyone, including itself.

Yet the most revealing part of this myth emerges when someone finally steps back and notices how much of the busyness is self-created. Unmade decisions, unclear communication, delayed approvals, and unexplored options accumulate into unnecessary emergencies that could have been prevented with a moment of foresight. The team learns to anticipate these patterns before the leader does. They brace for the fallout. They predict the scramble. They recognize the difference between real urgency and the artificial urgency created by poor planning. And somewhere along the way, they begin to wonder how much further they could go if the person guiding them was capable of slowing down long enough to lead with intention.

But even in that frustration, there is a deeper clarity waiting to be uncovered. Watching a leader drown in their own busyness teaches you what leadership should never become—and what it must become if it hopes to thrive. It teaches you that progress requires stillness. That decisions require space. That leadership is less about managing time and more about mastering attention. And as this awareness settles in, you begin to see that the real work of leadership is not in doing everything, but in seeing clearly enough to choose what actually matters.

Busy leaders rarely understand this distinction, because in their world, movement feels like proof of their value. But transformational leaders learn that busyness is often a symptom of avoidance—avoiding strategy, avoiding accountability, avoiding the vulnerability of slowing down long enough to think deeply and act deliberately. True leadership asks for something harder than constant motion; it asks for clarity, discipline, and the courage to let go of everything that masquerades as importance but contributes nothing to the future.

And perhaps that is where the quiet transformation begins— not in judging the leader who mistakes activity for progress, but in recognizing the opportunity to lead differently. To create spaces where thinking is not an afterthought but a requirement. To design systems that prevent chaos instead of responding to it. To build a culture where progress is measured not by how much is done, but by how much is moved forward. Because once a leader understands that busyness is not the measure of their worth, they become free to pursue something far more powerful: the kind of progress that changes the work, the team, and ultimately, themselves.

"A leader who can't see past today will always confuse urgency with direction."

CHAPTER 2

The Leader Who Can't See Past Today

"The future arrives too soon for those who have not prepared for it."

— John C. Maxwell

There is a particular heaviness that settles in a workplace when the person in charge cannot think beyond the moment directly in front of them. At first, it looks like harmless short-term focus—answering what's urgent, reacting to whatever noise happens to be loudest that day, addressing problems as they land instead of as they form. But over time, the pattern becomes impossible to ignore. Nothing is ever anticipated. Nothing is ever prevented. Nothing is ever understood deeply enough to be avoided the next time. The leader moves from task to task as if leadership is nothing more than a long string of immediate reactions, and everyone beneath them begins to feel the consequences of a vision that ends at the edge of the current hour.

You notice the signs before you fully admit them. Projects are rushed without direction, then stalled without explanation. Decisions are made without context, then undone without accountability. Plans are created without purpose, then abandoned without learning anything from the failure. Each day becomes a series of disconnected actions, none of which point toward a future. And slowly, almost quietly, you realize the truth: this is not leadership—it is survival. The leader is not looking ahead because they don't know how. They respond because they cannot think. They do because they cannot design. They "lead" because they were placed in the role, not because they ever learned how to carry it.

Still, you try to compensate. You fill in the gaps, anticipate the risks, and prepare for what they refuse to see. You ask the questions they never consider, raise the concerns they don't understand, and provide the rationale they didn't realize they needed. A part of you hopes your example will inspire them to think differently, to widen their perspective, to recognize the value of looking beyond the surface. But instead of rising to meet you, they retreat deeper into the comfort of immediacy, confusing your clarity for challenge and your foresight for threat.

And this is where the frustration becomes personal. Because you do not lead the way they do. You do not fear hard decisions or hide from uncomfortable truths. You do not push busywork forward to avoid accountability. You do not accept dysfunction simply because it is familiar. You question, not to disrupt but to strengthen. You push back, not to resist but to refine. You make decisions with intention, not avoidance. And every time your integrity touches their insecurity, they treat your leadership as a complication instead of an asset.

Yet even as you carry this tension, another realization begins to form—a realization that explains more than it condemns. Leaders who cannot see past today are not simply unskilled; they are overwhelmed by the very idea of tomorrow. Vision requires imagination. Strategy requires confidence. Foresight requires a willingness to be held accountable for the consequences of what you decide. And some people do not have the emotional stability, professional grounding, or self-awareness required to think that far ahead. They manage the moment because the moment is the only place where they feel safe.

> *"When a leader fears long-term thinking, everyone beneath them pays or the consequences they refuse to see."*

But when a leader cannot lift their eyes to the horizon, the team is forced to live in a world that never moves beyond the present. Work becomes cyclical, not progressive. Conversations become repetitive, not developmental. Effort becomes exhausting, not empowering. The environment slowly closes in on itself until innovation feels impossible and growth feels optional. And in that stagnation, something inside you begins to ache—not because you expect perfection, but because you know how much potential is being wasted by a leadership mindset that refuses to expand.

You also begin to see why your presence unsettles them. A leader who cannot see past today will always struggle with a team member who can see tomorrow, next month, and next year with ease. Your questions expose what they haven't considered. Your clarity highlights what they have ignored. Your rationale reveals where their decisions lack grounding. Your pushback shows where they have confused authority with direction. And because they cannot process the discomfort of that reflection, they respond by shrinking the space around you, hoping that if they narrow your impact, they can avoid facing their own limitations.

But even in their resistance, you never stop doing what true leaders do: preparing for what's coming. You think ahead because it is who you are, not because it is who they taught you to be. You look for patterns, not because it is required, but because it is instinctual. You provide justification, not because you must defend yourself, but because you respect the weight of decisions. And in every moment where they choose the immediacy of today, you quietly hold the blueprint for a future they have yet to imagine.

Over time, this contrast becomes the deepest revelation of all. Leadership is not proven by position, or authority, or proximity to power. Leadership is proven by perspective. By vision. By the willingness to look beyond what is comfortable or convenient and choose what is responsible and true. Anyone can respond to a moment. But not everyone can guide one. And the more you witness the difference, the more you understand that leadership is not a title granted from above—it is a calling recognized from within.

And perhaps that is why your frustration runs so deep. You are a leader in a place where leadership has not been required, expected, or modeled in any meaningful way. You see what they cannot. You understand what they avoid. You prepare for what they refuse to acknowledge. And in that quiet, undeniable separation, the truth becomes clear: leadership is not about seeing what is happening today. It is about seeing what will happen if nothing changes.

"Reactive leadership costs more than money — it drains clarity, trust, and the will to keep trying."

CHAPTER 3

The Cost of Reaction-Based Leadership

"An ounce of prevention is worth a pound of cure."

— *Benjamin Franklin*

There is a hidden cost that builds quietly in workplaces led by people who cannot think beyond the urgency of the moment. At first, it shows up as small inefficiencies—tasks repeated unnecessarily, documents recreated without reason, meetings called to discuss problems that already have answers. These moments seem harmless on their own, just minor inconveniences in the flow of work. But as they accumulate, they reveal a deeper truth: reaction-based leadership does not simply create chaos; it consumes the time, energy, and potential of everyone forced to operate beneath it.

You see this most clearly in the constant reinvention that becomes normalized under leaders who never slow down long enough to comprehend what already exists. They request information that has been written, reviewed, and archived multiple times. They ask for slides despite having nine versions already sitting on their desktop. They call for summaries that live in documents they never opened. They panic at questions the team has already answered. And because they cannot connect today's ask to yesterday's work, they manufacture emergencies that demand immediate attention—emergencies that would not exist if they engaged with the material they claim to oversee.

Over time, the team learns that the chaos is not situational; it is structural. Every new request begins with urgency, not clarity. Every project begins with confusion, not direction. Every deadline is treated as a crisis, even when the work is familiar. And because the leader never integrates the knowledge they receive, the team must constantly rebuild from scratch, offering the same explanations, the same context, the same documents, the same slides—all while knowing that none of it will be remembered the next time. It becomes a cycle so predictable that frustration turns into resignation.

What makes this cycle so damaging is not just the wasted effort, but the emotional weight of watching your work evaporate each time the leader forgets it exists. There is a particular exhaustion that comes from having to constantly recreate what should have been preserved, from answering questions that should have been understood, from responding to panic that should never have arisen. It is the fatigue of pouring clarity into a container that cannot hold it, of offering structure to someone who refuses to stand still long enough to recognize its value. And in that fatigue, you begin to understand that reaction-based leadership is not simply inefficient—it is deeply demoralizing.

This demoralization grows sharper when you recognize how differently you navigate the same work. While they scramble, you analyze. While they panic, you prioritize. While they request the tenth version of a deck, you quietly remember the data from the second and the examples from the fifth. Your mind works in patterns, in threads, in continuity. You see how information connects, how decisions ripple outward, how today's work becomes tomorrow's foundation. But under reaction-based leadership, that strength becomes a burden—because every time you try to bring coherence, the leader drags the work back into fragmentation.

And the fragmentation is not accidental; it is a byproduct of how they process the world. Leaders who operate in constant reaction cannot build systems because systems require vision, discipline, and comprehension. They cannot create consistency because consistency demands memory, context, and emotional steadiness. They cannot provide guidance because guidance requires an understanding of the path ahead. So instead, they rely on motion—rapid, urgent, chaotic motion—to distract from the absence of direction. And because their panic feels like activity, they assume they are leading.

But the team knows better. The team feels the cost in the hours spent correcting avoidable errors, in the late nights fixing slides that already exist in a better version, in the rework that piles up because the leader didn't read, didn't listen, or didn't pause long enough to understand. They feel it in the meetings where decisions are made without context, then reversed without explanation. They feel it in the tension of trying to preserve quality in an environment where speed is valued more than sense. And they feel it most deeply in the erosion of trust—the slow, quiet acceptance that no matter how well they perform, the leadership above them will continue pulling the work backward.

Yet even as the cost reveals itself in these tangible frustrations, another truth begins to surface—one that is harder to face but impossible to deny. Reaction-based leadership doesn't only damage the work; it damages the people. It conditions high performers to lower their expectations, not because they lack ambition, but because ambition becomes unsustainable in an environment that refuses to evolve. It teaches talented individuals to stop offering ideas, not because they lack insight, but because insight goes nowhere when the leader cannot see beyond the present moment. And it slowly wears down the confidence of those who know the most, because they spend so much time compensating for leadership that knows the least.

That is the quiet tragedy of this kind of leadership: it wastes potential, not through malice but through limitation. It shrinks the space where innovation could thrive. It suppresses the clarity that could simplify everything. It replaces learning with repetition and progress with exhaustion. And in doing so, it forces the true leaders—the ones who think, anticipate, and understand—to live beneath the weight of someone else's confusion.

> ***"Every time a leader chooses reaction over preparation, the team pays for the mistake twice — once in effort, and again in morale."***

But even in that heaviness, there is a revelation waiting for those who can see it. The contrast between reaction and leadership becomes undeniable, and once you've lived through enough cycles of chaos, you begin to recognize your own value with startling clarity. You see that your ability to synthesize information is not ordinary. Your instinct for patterns is not common. Your willingness to push back is not rebellion but responsibility. And your calm, reasoned approach is not a personality trait—it is leadership in its truest form.

So, perhaps that is the greatest cost of reaction-based leadership: not the wasted hours or the repeated work, but the way it reveals who the real leaders are—and how deeply they are needed in places that do not yet know how to recognize them.

"When the leader becomes the bottleneck, progress isn't slowed — it stops."

CHAPTER 4

The Bottleneck Effect

"There is nothing so useless as doing efficiently what should not be done at all."

— *Peter Drucker*

There is a moment in every dysfunctional organization when the work stops flowing the way it should. At first, you can't identify the exact point of blockage; you just sense delays where there shouldn't be delays, confusion where there should be clarity, hesitation where there should be movement. Everything feels slightly slower, slightly heavier, slightly more complicated than the work itself requires. And as you begin to trace the path of each task—where it starts, where it travels, where it stalls—you notice something both unmistakable and deeply troubling: all roads lead back to the same person.

The bottleneck is not the system. It is not the workload. It is not the team. It is the leader.

The realization settles quietly at first, arriving more as an intuition than a conclusion. You begin to see that every decision waits for their approval, even when they lack the context to make it. Every deliverable requires their input, even when that input adds no value. Every project pauses at the exact moment it reaches their desk, not because they are intentionally slowing the work, but because they do not have the capacity to move it forward. And instead of admitting that they are overwhelmed or out of their depth, they step deeper into the illusion of control—tightening their grip on every detail, while unknowingly becoming the very obstruction they believe they are preventing.

The irony is painful. Leaders who fear losing control often create the chaos that makes control impossible. They micromanage decisions they don't understand, insert themselves into processes they don't follow, and demand updates for the sake of assurance rather than insight. And because they do not have the clarity needed to provide direction, they stall, revise, or reverse decisions in ways that compound the delay. Work that should flow becomes work that must wait, and the team learns to brace themselves for the inevitable moment when progress hits the wall of unclear leadership.

What makes this bottleneck effect so corrosive is not just the slowdown itself, but the emotional impact it has on those who rely on the leader to advance the work. You feel the drag of every unnecessary pause, not just as an inconvenience, but as a distortion of your own momentum. You feel yourself expending twice the effort to counter the friction created by someone who should be reducing it. And as the delays accumulate, you begin to internalize a subtle but significant truth: the organization will only move as fast as its slowest decision-maker, and unfortunately, that decision-maker sits at the top.

Yet even as this recognition grows clearer, another layer of complexity emerges—because leaders who become bottlenecks rarely acknowledge the role they play in slowing everything down. Instead, they project the delay onto the work itself. They call the project "complex," even when it isn't. They blame the team for not moving fast enough, even when the team is sprinting. They point to resource constraints, competing priorities, or sudden escalations, anything to avoid facing the uncomfortable reality that the true obstruction is their own inability to process the information required to lead.

"A bottleneck doesn't appear at the bottom of an organization — it forms

at the point where decisions stop moving."

This denial creates a dangerous ripple. Teams begin building workarounds to avoid the bottleneck—drafting shadow processes, redefining responsibilities, or quietly making decisions the leader should have made weeks earlier. The goal is never rebellion; it is survival. People want to move the work forward, and when leadership cannot do it, they create the momentum themselves. But the more they compensate, the more invisible the bottleneck becomes, allowing the leader to believe that the system is functioning, when in truth it is functioning in spite of them.

And this is where the emotional exhaustion reaches its peak. High performers feel themselves pulled into a never-ending cycle of rescuing work that should not need rescuing. They become the de facto decision-makers, the unofficial strategists, the unacknowledged architects of coherence. They carry not only their assigned tasks, but the weight of the leader's paralysis. And in that burden, they begin to recognize something that both validates them and quietly breaks them: the organization works only because they do.

But even in this grim clarity, another insight begins to take shape—one that exposes the root of the bottleneck more honestly than frustration ever could. Leaders who block the flow of work are not always malicious or indifferent; sometimes they are simply unprepared for the level of thinking leadership requires. They are overwhelmed by information they don't understand, intimidated by decisions they don't feel equipped to make, and terrified of being held responsible for outcomes they cannot predict. And instead of seeking clarity, they retreat into control. Instead of empowering others, they slow them down. Instead of lifting the work higher, they hold it tightly, hoping it will eventually make sense.

The tragedy is that leadership was never meant to be a place of fear. It was meant to be a vantage point—a position that allows someone to see farther, think deeper, and guide others toward what lies ahead. But when fear is the foundation, the vantage point becomes a blind spot. The leader sees less, not more. The work moves slower, not faster. The team grows quieter, not stronger. And the bottleneck expands until it becomes the defining characteristic of the organization itself.

Yet even in the midst of this dysfunction, something powerful happens for the people who can see it clearly. The contrast between obstruction and leadership becomes a mirror. It reflects what you will never become. It reminds you why you think differently. It clarifies your instincts, your patience, your capacity, and your endurance. And with each cycle of delay you navigate, you feel the unmistakable formation of something steady inside you—a deep, grounded certainty that real leadership is not about holding the work tightly, but about clearing the path so it can move.

And that is perhaps the quiet gift hidden inside the bottleneck effect. Watching a leader block the very progress they are supposed to champion teaches you, with painful precision, what it means to lead from a place of abundance rather than fear. It teaches you that clarity is not a luxury, but a responsibility. It teaches you that comprehension is not optional, but essential. And most importantly, it teaches you that leadership is not the act of standing in front—it is the act of getting out of the way.

"Short-sighted leadership is rarely about skill — it is almost always about fear."

CHAPTER 5

The Psychology Behind Short-Sighted Leaders

"Nothing in life is to be feared, it is only to be understood."

— *Marie Curie*

There comes a point when the frustration shifts from the surface to something deeper. You stop reacting to the symptoms—the rushed projects, the unnecessary emergencies, the recycled mistakes—and begin asking a quieter question beneath it all: *Why do they lead this way?* Because no one wakes up intending to create confusion or derail progress, yet somehow the pattern repeats itself with a consistency that reveals more than circumstance. What starts as irritation becomes inquiry, and inquiry uncovers a kind of truth you wish you had recognized sooner.

Short-sighted leaders rarely operate from confidence. Their decisions are shaped far more by insecurity than by intention. On the outside, they may appear decisive or commanding, but internally they often carry the uneasy sense that they are not fully equipped for the role they've been given. Vision requires certainty; they do not have it. Strategy requires comprehension; they struggle to maintain it. Anticipation requires a steady internal landscape; theirs is unsettled. So they cling to the present moment because the future feels too vast, too unpredictable, too exposing. Reacting becomes safer than thinking.

This fear of exposure appears in subtle ways. They avoid reading deeply because depth reveals what they don't understand. They request information at the last minute because planning ahead would force them to confront gaps in their knowledge. They micromanage the small details because the big picture overwhelms them. Each behavior is a way to stay close to what feels controllable, even if the cost is clarity, direction, and team trust. The leader isn't trying to make things harder; they are trying to survive their own discomfort.

Another layer sits beneath this: many of these leaders were promoted for reasons unrelated to leadership. Longevity, loyalty, visibility, or convenience often lift people into positions they were never trained or prepared to carry. The skills that brought them upward—responsiveness, compliance, familiarity with the system—are not the skills needed to guide others with vision. When they reach the level where comprehension and foresight become essential, they find themselves standing on unfamiliar ground. Instead of growing into the role, they try to shrink the role until it fits them.

The result is a leader who relies on urgency as a substitute for direction. Urgency feels active, even when it is unproductive. It creates the illusion of momentum, even when nothing is advancing. It masks uncertainty because speed distracts from the absence of understanding. Over time, urgency becomes their shield: if everything is a crisis, then no one questions why the leader isn't thinking further ahead. Chaos becomes a kind of camouflage, hiding confusion behind motion.

There is also the matter of accountability. Thinking ahead requires committing to a path. Committing to a path creates responsibility for what follows. Leaders who fear being held accountable often avoid decisions until the last possible moment, hoping that circumstances will force their hand or that someone else will step in with the clarity they lack. This pattern doesn't appear as fear; it appears as delay, revision, or sudden bursts of frenzied direction that fall apart as quickly as they form. Yet beneath every stalled project lies the same truth: the leader was not ready to take ownership of what the decision required.

Short-sighted leaders tend to process information in fragments rather than connections. They rely on isolated facts, single requests, and immediate demands because they have not built a mental map of the broader landscape. Without that map, everything feels new, even when it isn't. Every ask feels separate, even when the answers already exist. Every task feels urgent, even when the work has been done nine times before. The leader's inability to see continuity becomes the team's burden, forcing others to compensate for a pattern the leader does not recognize in themselves.

Despite all of this, it is important to acknowledge that many of these leaders are not intentionally harmful. They are overwhelmed. Their fear of being inadequate creates behaviors that protect them in the moment but damage the organization over time. It is difficult to admit you don't understand something you're expected to lead. It is difficult to ask questions when you believe those questions will expose you. It is difficult to step back and reflect when reflection threatens the identity you've built around appearing capable. Their avoidance is, in its own way, a protective instinct.

Recognizing the psychology behind these behaviors does not excuse the harm they cause, but it does explain why change rarely comes from them. Growth requires self-awareness, and self-awareness requires stillness—the very thing they avoid. To evolve, they would need to confront what is uncomfortable: the gaps in their knowledge, the fears that drive their urgency, the inconsistencies in their leadership, the patterns others have been carrying on their behalf. Until that reckoning happens, the cycle continues.

"A leader who avoids uncertainty will always choose comfort over clarity — and the team will pay for that choice."

For those who understand what the work *should* look like, this realization is bittersweet. It becomes clear that the leader is not the villain of the story; they are the limitation. They do not slow the team out of malice but out of fear. They do not resist clarity because they want confusion but because clarity would expose how unprepared they truly feel. Once you see this dynamic clearly, you stop expecting them to transform into someone they are not. You adjust your expectations not out of cynicism, but out of wisdom.

And that wisdom changes how you interpret their actions. The frantic requests, the last-minute slides, the sudden meetings, the hesitation to connect dots—all of it reflects an inner landscape that never found its footing. You may still be frustrated, but the frustration shifts shape. It becomes a recognition of what leadership requires, and why so many people struggle to embody it. Vision is not a task; it is a temperament. Comprehension is not a skill; it is a discipline. Leadership is not a title; it is a way of thinking long before it becomes a way of directing others.

In that clarity, something profound happens. You begin to trust your own instincts more deeply. You recognize that your ability to anticipate, synthesize, and connect information is not just a strength—it is leadership in its most honest form. You see how naturally you do the things others find overwhelming, and you understand why the work always seems to rise to meet you. The psychology of short-sighted leadership reveals, by contrast, the psychology of those who are truly called to lead.

"Visionary leadership is not about seeing more — it's about seeing sooner."

CHAPTER 6

Visionary Leadership—What It Actually Looks Like

"Management is about arranging and telling. Leadership is about nurturing and enhancing."

— *Tom Peters*

There is a quiet moment in every professional journey when you finally understand that leadership is not defined by authority, position, or the ability to deliver polished presentations on demand. Leadership reveals itself in something far rarer: the consistent ability to see beyond what is happening right now. For a long time, this truth hides behind the noise of workplace culture, where urgency is mistaken for importance and speed is mistaken for direction. But eventually, after navigating enough disorganized systems and short-sighted decisions, the real shape of leadership comes into view.

Visionary leaders do not move faster than everyone else; they move with purpose. Their presence has a steadiness to it, a sense that they are tuned into a larger rhythm than the daily grind. While others scramble to assemble last-minute slides, the visionary already knows where every piece of information lives. Not because they have a superhuman memory, but because they build systems that make chaos unnecessary. Clarity is their baseline, not their reward. It becomes obvious, once you've experienced both types of leadership, how different the air feels around someone who actually thinks ahead.

The most distinguishing trait of a visionary is their relationship with information. They absorb it, not collect it. They read to understand, not to complete a task. They make connections instinctively, noticing how one document informs another, how one meeting shapes the next, how one decision ripples through a project months later. They do not treat information as isolated events; they treat it as a landscape. In their hands, complexity becomes coherence. This is why their teams feel grounded—they are guided by someone who sees what others miss.

Visionary leaders also anticipate patterns before anyone else realizes a pattern exists. They notice subtle shifts in behavior, emerging risks, and recurring concerns long before these issues grow into crises. Their foresight is not mystical; it is simply attentive. They pay attention to the small signs that most people overlook—the tension in a conversation, the gap in a plan, the inconsistency in a narrative. While short-sighted leaders react to fires, visionaries identify the spark. They do not wait for the flames to rise before they begin thinking about prevention.

Another defining trait is their ease with decision-making. Visionary leaders do not rush decisions, but they do not fear them either. They understand that every choice, large or small, becomes part of a larger trajectory. Because they see the trajectory clearly, they move with confidence. Even when they are unsure, they seek clarity rather than hiding behind urgency. They ask the right questions, gather the right context, and take responsibility for the outcome. Accountability does not intimidate them; it steadies them. This courage is what allows their teams to operate without fear.

There is also a unique generosity among leaders who think this way. Visionaries do not hoard information or position themselves as the sole source of authority. They share context freely because they want people to understand, not just comply. They invite insights from others because they see leadership as a collective intelligence, not a hierarchy of ego. Their confidence leaves room for collaboration. Their clarity creates space for growth. People do not just follow visionaries—they learn from them.

Perhaps the most remarkable quality of visionary leadership is its emotional grounding. These leaders are rarely shaken by the unexpected. They do not translate every request into a crisis. They do not transfer their anxiety to the team. Even in uncertainty, they maintain a calm center because they trust the process they've built and the people they've empowered. This steadiness is not the absence of pressure; it is the mastery of it. And it changes the entire emotional climate of a workplace. When the leader is calm, the team breathes.

You begin to recognize, through contrast, how rare this kind of leadership truly is. It stands out precisely because it is not loud. Visionaries do not need to schedule unnecessary meetings or request repeated versions of the same deck to prove they are engaged. Their work speaks for itself. Their decisions reflect thought, not panic. Their teams move efficiently not because they are pushed, but because they are guided. In their presence, you feel the difference between being managed and being led.

As you observe these qualities more closely, another truth becomes impossible to ignore: some people step into leadership because they want authority, while others step into leadership because they want responsibility. The visionary falls into the second category. They are not drawn to the role for its prestige or visibility; they are drawn to it because they understand the weight of guiding others. Their motivation is not control—it is stewardship. This distinction shapes every choice they make.

"Visionary leaders design the path before the team ever has to walk it."

Over time, working with or near leaders who think this way can feel like a revelation. Suddenly, the chaos you once assumed was inevitable disappears. The constant rework evaporates. The panic quiets. The pressure becomes productive instead of draining. You are reminded of what work can feel like when it is led by someone who sees not only the task in front of them, but the direction beneath it. You begin to understand that the difference between visionary leadership and reaction-based leadership is not subtle; it is transformative.

The more you witness this contrast, the more clearly you see your own instincts reflected back to you. The parts of yourself that once felt like "too much"—the questions, the foresight, the connections, the need for clarity—suddenly appear as strengths rather than complications. You realize you have been thinking like a leader long before anyone gave you permission to say so. Vision recognizes vision, even when it shows up quietly in the edge of a room where no one is paying attention.

Slowly, you realize that is the greatest revelation of all: visionary leadership is not something people learn after they receive a title. It is something they carry long before anyone notices. It shows up in how they think, how they listen, how they process information, and how they choose to move through the world. Titles may announce leaders, but vision reveals them.

"Cycles exhaust people. Systems empower them."

CHAPTER 7

Leaders Who Build Systems Instead of Cycles

"In preparing for battle I have always found that plans are useless, but planning is indispensable."

— *Dwight D. Eisenhower*

There comes a point when you realize that the most powerful leaders are not the ones who fix problems the fastest, but the ones who design the work in a way that prevents those problems from returning. It is a quiet distinction, one easily overlooked in workplaces where urgency is celebrated and reactivity is mistaken for competence. Yet over time, you begin to observe a pattern: leaders who build systems create progress, while leaders who create cycles keep everyone trapped in the same exhausting loop.

Leaders who operate through cycles often believe they are being responsive. They answer every request as it comes, address every issue as it arises, and react to every challenge with immediate intensity. On the surface, this looks like engagement. It looks like involvement. It looks like someone who is deeply committed to the work. But beneath that performance lies a repeating pattern: nothing is ever truly resolved. Problems reappear in slightly different forms, errors resurface months after being "fixed," and the team finds itself revisiting the same conversations over and over again. The cycle feels endless because it is.

In contrast, leaders who build systems approach the work from a very different angle. Instead of asking, *How do we solve this today?* they ask, *How do we make sure this doesn't happen again?* They examine patterns, not moments. They look for root causes, not symptoms. They design processes that carry clarity, reduce confusion, and ensure that the team's energy flows toward outcomes rather than repairs. Their questions guide the organization toward prevention, not repetition. This shift may seem small, but its impact is profound.

You notice it most clearly in how they respond to problems. A leader trapped in cycles rushes to put out the fire. A system-builder steps back long enough to understand why the fire started in the first place. The first relies on urgency; the second relies on structure. The difference becomes obvious when you observe how the team feels after a problem is addressed. With a cycle-driven leader, the relief is temporary—everyone knows the issue will surface again, and probably soon. With a system-building leader, the relief is real. The solution holds. The team moves forward without the weight of anticipation.

System-builders carry a different mindset about information as well. They track what has been created, what has been learned, and how each piece of work fits into the larger landscape. Documents are not one-time deliverables to them; they are building blocks. Presentations are not throwaway tasks; they are reusable assets. Decisions are not isolated events; they are part of a pattern. This awareness creates efficiency that is almost invisible—tasks finish faster, questions are answered with clarity, direction feels easy to follow. Stability becomes the natural byproduct of thoughtful design.

Cycle-driven leaders, on the other hand, often lose track of what already exists. They reinvent material that could have been repurposed. They request new versions of work simply because they cannot recall the old ones. They create urgency around tasks that should be simple, because they have no internal map of the information that surrounds them. Their teams spend countless hours recreating what should have been preserved. The cycle becomes exhausting, not because the work is hard, but because the leader has created an environment where progress resets itself every week.

Once you have worked with someone who builds systems, it becomes impossible to view cycles as normal. The contrast reveals just how wasteful the loop truly is. You start recognizing how many of your own skills—organization, coherence, anticipation, pattern recognition—are actually forms of system-building. These abilities are not simply preferences or habits; they are the foundation of sustainable leadership. They allow you to guide work in a way that frees people from scrambling and gives them space to actually perform. Stability, in this context, is not passive. It is the product of intentional structure.

Another powerful indicator of a system-building leader is their relationship with time. They do not rush toward completion; they move toward continuity. They think beyond the moment and build for what comes next. Their decisions consider the future of the team, the longevity of the project, and the health of the system. They respect the time of others because they respect the importance of the work. Contrast this with leaders stuck in cycles, who consume time as if it were endless—demanding last-minute updates, rewriting documents unnecessarily, and asking for repeated efforts that drain both morale and momentum.

The emotional difference between these two leadership styles cannot be overstated. In a cycle-driven environment, people learn to brace themselves for inefficiencies. They expect confusion, anticipate rework, and expend mental energy navigating obstacles that should not exist. Their creativity shrinks under the weight of constant repetition. But within a system-led environment, people flourish. They feel grounded, supported, and trusted. They know what success looks like and how to achieve it. The work becomes smoother not because the tasks are easier, but because the leadership has removed unnecessary obstacles.

Eventually, the contrast becomes a kind of internal compass, revealing not only what kind of leader you work best under but what kind of leader you are becoming. When you recognize that stability, clarity, and continuity come naturally to you, something inside settles. You see that your instinct to ask questions, plan ahead, connect information, and streamline processes is not a burden—it is vision in motion. You build systems almost by reflex because you understand that progress should not feel like starting over every day.

This awareness changes how you interpret your own value. It becomes clear that system-builders do not simply perform tasks; they elevate organizations. They create an environment where success becomes predictable instead of accidental. They steward the work in a way that honors both the mission and the people contributing to it. Most importantly, they break the cycle that keeps teams exhausted and replace it with a structure that allows everyone to move forward with intention.

By the time this understanding settles, you can no longer be fooled by the noise of busyness or the theatrics of urgency. You know, with steady certainty, that leaders who build systems will always outperform those who create cycles. One keeps people trapped. The other sets them free.

"Reactive leaders rebuild the same fire every week; systems-builders ensure it never ignites in the first place."

"Short-sighted leaders react to the first consequence. Visionaries prepare for the third."

CHAPTER 8

The Second-Order Consequence Mindset

"The significant problems we face cannot be solved at the same level of thinking we were at when we created them."

— Albert Einstein

There is a quiet brilliance in leaders who think past the first impact of a decision. Most people see only what happens immediately—the next step, the next deliverable, the next email that must be answered. They respond to what is directly in front of them because it feels concrete and manageable. But visionary leaders live in a different mental landscape. They understand that every action creates a ripple, and those ripples often matter more than the initial splash. Leadership, to them, is not about managing the moment—it is about shaping what the moment will become.

This mindset shows itself in the way they pause before deciding. The pause is not hesitation; it is evaluation. While others rush to resolve the pressure of now, the visionary quietly examines what will unfold tomorrow, next week, or next quarter as a result of whatever path they choose. They consider who will be affected, what resources will be strained, where confusion may arise, and how the decision aligns with the long arc of the work. Because they look beyond the obvious, their choices tend to lift the organization rather than burden it.

You can feel this difference in how they interpret problems. A short-sighted leader sees a missed deadline and asks who dropped the ball. A visionary sees a missed deadline and wonders what failed upstream—what process, what assumption, what gap in clarity contributed to the delay. The first looks for a culprit; the second looks for a cause. That shift in perspective transforms how they lead. Instead of creating environments where people fear mistakes, they create environments where learning is valued and systems evolve. They understand that the surface issue is rarely the root.

Second-order thinking becomes most visible when decisions involve pressure. In moments where urgency tempts leaders to choose whatever solves the problem fastest, the visionary remains anchored in long-term stability. They recognize that a quick fix may ease today's discomfort while creating a greater burden tomorrow. Their question is never simply, *Will this work now?* but rather, *What happens after this works? What happens if it doesn't? What happens next?* This habit of looking forward protects the team from unnecessary cycles of rework and ensures that progress is genuine rather than performative.

This mindset also reveals itself in how visionary leaders handle communication. They do not share information haphazardly or call meetings simply to relieve their own uncertainty. They think through the effect their message will have on the room. They consider how every word may influence action, morale, clarity, or confusion. They know that communication is not just about speaking—it is about guiding. Poor leaders talk to offload pressure; strong leaders speak to shape direction. Their awareness of the ripple effect makes their words weighty, intentional, and steadying.

"Most leaders make decisions for today; great leaders make decisions for the chain of tomorrows that follow."

Another powerful element of second-order thinking is the way it supports resilience. While surface-level leaders are constantly surprised by problems they didn't foresee, visionaries are rarely caught off guard. They are not clairvoyant—they are attentive. They notice early signs, shifting dynamics, and unresolved tensions that hint at what is coming. Their ability to predict consequences allows them to prepare the team rather than react with panic. In their presence, challenges feel manageable because someone has already thought through the implications before the crisis fully appears.

This is why teams under visionary leadership tend to trust their leaders deeply. They feel guided, not tossed around. They sense that decisions come from a place of understanding rather than impulse. They are not asked to absorb the fallout of poorly considered choices. Instead, they are given clarity, context, and direction rooted in foresight. The work may still be difficult, but it unfolds in a way that feels purposeful rather than chaotic.

Over time, the distinction between first-order and second-order thinkers becomes unmistakable. Leaders who focus only on immediate outcomes create environments filled with sudden shifts, repeated errors, and unnecessary complications. They unintentionally design workplaces where every week feels like a reset. In contrast, leaders who think beyond the moment create a smoothness in the workflow—a sense that the organization is being carried forward rather than dragged along. Momentum becomes sustainable instead of sporadic.

This contrast also brings into focus something deeply personal: your own instinct to think ahead is not a quirk. It is a form of intelligence that many people never develop. When you look at a decision, you naturally see the branches of possibility—the way one choice can strengthen a project or undermine it, the way a misunderstanding today can create confusion months later, the way clarity now can save hours of rework down the road. That instinct is the mark of someone who was born to lead, not because of position but because of perception.

By the time you fully recognize this difference, second-order thinking no longer feels like an advanced skill—it feels like the standard leadership never taught. You understand with quiet certainty that true leadership requires a mind that can hold both the present and the future at once. It requires someone who understands that every decision is a seed. Some seeds sprout progress. Others sprout problems. Visionaries know the difference before the ground even shifts.

In that understanding, you begin to step more fully into your own leadership identity. You realize that your ability to anticipate consequences is not a burden on the team—it is a gift to it. You see that your foresight is not overthinking; it is strategic thinking. And you recognize that leadership is not about reacting well to what happens, but about guiding others toward what could happen if the right choices are made.

That realization changes everything.

"Leadership is felt long before it is understood."

CHAPTER 9

Experiencing Different Leader Types

"We do not see things as they are; we see them as we are."

— *Anaïs Nin*

There is a moment in every career when you finally feel the difference between being managed and being led. It doesn't happen in a dramatic scene or a single conversation; it arrives quietly, often in the middle of an ordinary workday, when you realize how differently your mind and body respond depending on who stands at the front. The contrast is so sharp, so undeniable, that once you experience it, you cannot unsee it. You carry the memory of each type of leader with you because the feeling they create stays long after the project ends.

Working under a short-sighted leader feels like living inside a storm that never fully passes. Even on calm days, you brace yourself without realizing it. You anticipate the sudden email, the abrupt shift in direction, the last-minute request for information that already exists. Your nervous system remains half-engaged, waiting for the moment when their lack of preparation becomes your emergency. The work is not inherently chaotic, but their approach makes it feel unpredictable. You learn to scan for potential fire drills instead of focusing on meaningful progress.

The emotional weight of this environment settles slowly. You begin doubting your own clarity because the leader has none. You hesitate before offering insight because it will likely be ignored, forgotten, or misinterpreted. You learn that excellence doesn't matter if leadership cannot recognize it, and efficiency doesn't matter if leadership keeps recycling old confusion. Over time, you feel yourself shrinking your instincts just to survive their reactions. It becomes harder to think creatively when every thought is interrupted by unnecessary urgency.

There is also a particular loneliness that forms under this kind of leadership. You know the work could be better, smoother, smarter. You see the path forward, but you are tethered to someone who cannot see beyond the day. When they panic, the panic becomes yours. When they misunderstand, you are forced to rewrite what should have been read. When they forget, you redo what was already done. The cycle wears you down not because you lack resilience, but because you are carrying weight they were meant to hold.

Yet the contrast becomes startling the first time you work with a visionary leader. Something in you relaxes before you can name why. Their presence does not demand your vigilance; it invites your best thinking. You feel safe enough to contribute ideas without bracing for confusion. You trust that when they ask for information, it is because they intend to use it thoughtfully. There is no frantic energy, no self-inflicted emergencies, no sense that every request must be handled as if the whole project rests in a single moment.

Under visionary leadership, the work feels purposeful. You can breathe. You can plan. You can think several steps ahead because your leader already is. Clarity becomes the norm, not the exception. They give you context instead of commands. They listen without defensiveness. They ask questions that show they understand the landscape, not just the tasks. In their presence, you rediscover the part of yourself that loves the work rather than enduring it.

The emotional shift is profound. Where reactive leaders drain you, visionary leaders replenish you. Where reactive leaders create tension, visionary leaders create direction. The same skills you once had to mute suddenly come alive. Your pattern recognition, your foresight, your desire to build something meaningful—these qualities no longer feel like burdens. You begin trusting them again because they finally have somewhere to land.

Over time, you recognize that visionary leadership creates an environment where people rise naturally. They are not pushed, threatened, or micromanaged. They are guided. They feel seen—not in a performative sense, but in a way that honors their capability. The team moves as a whole rather than as a collection of individuals scrambling to compensate. Momentum builds without chaos. Productivity emerges without pressure. The difference is unmistakable.

What surprises you most is how quickly your confidence returns when the leadership above you is steady. You start offering ideas you once kept to yourself. You reach for higher-quality work because you know it will be understood, not wasted. You rediscover ambition in places where exhaustion had taken root. It becomes clear that the right leadership doesn't just shape the work—it shapes the people doing the work.

Eventually, the two experiences sit side by side in your memory. You remember the heaviness of working under someone whose vision stops at the edge of the moment, and you remember the ease of working under someone who can see beyond the horizon. The contrast teaches you more about leadership than any training ever could. It shows you that leadership is not a personality trait or a title; it is an energy. One drains, one strengthens. One shrinks potential, one awakens it.

And through this contrast, you learn something essential about yourself. The reason the reactive leader felt suffocating is because you were built for something larger. You understand the work differently. You see the patterns, the direction, the consequences. This clarity does not come from training—it comes from who you are. Working under each type of leader reveals this truth in different ways. One experience dims your instincts until you feel disconnected from your own intelligence. The other sharpens them until you feel unmistakably aligned with your purpose.

By the time this realization settles, you no longer question your standards. You no longer wonder whether your expectations are unreasonable. You know, with grounded certainty, that real leadership is not measured by how loudly someone stands at the front of a room, but by how deeply they allow others to shine. And you carry that understanding with you because it shapes not only how you show up at work, but who you are becoming as a leader in your own right.

"A visionary feels the weight of a leader's gaps; a reactive follower feels the comfort of their pace."

> "You don't grow into leadership by accident — you grow into it by intention."

CHAPTER 10

Becoming the Leader Your Workplace Deserves

"The best way to make your dreams come true is to wake up."

— *Paul Valéry*

There comes a point in your journey when you realize that leadership is no longer something you're waiting to be granted. It is something you've already been living, quietly and consistently, long before anyone gives it a title. The clarity you bring to conversations, the foresight you carry into decisions, the systems you build instinctively—these are not traits you switch on when someone places authority in your hands. They are reflections of who you are. The challenge lies not in stepping into leadership, but in believing that you belong there.

This realization often arrives after years of navigating environments shaped by short-sighted thinking. At first, those experiences feel discouraging. You watch decisions unfold without direction, meetings spiral without purpose, and projects stall because someone above you cannot see past the day. You question whether the problem is the environment or your expectations. It takes time to understand that your frustration is not a sign of misalignment—it is a sign of readiness. You see the gaps because you know how to fill them. You recognize the limitations because you know what should exist in their place.

Once this truth settles, your relationship with leadership begins to shift. You stop looking for permission to speak up and start offering clarity because the work needs it. You stop shrinking your instincts to match the room and start trusting them because they consistently lead you toward insight. You stop assuming the leader must know something you don't and start recognizing when your perspective is the one the situation requires. Leadership moves from aspiration to identity, not because your circumstances changed, but because you finally acknowledge the abilities you've been carrying all along.

A leader who thinks this way does not wait for moments of crisis to offer guidance. You lead through prevention, not rescue. You anticipate the questions before they are asked.

You gather information before the gaps become visible. You create structure where there is drift, and direction where there is noise. Your leadership is not loud or performative. It shows up in the way you steady the environment, how you organize the chaos, and how you protect the work from unnecessary disruption. People may not always recognize the full extent of what you're doing, but they feel the difference almost immediately.

"Leadership begins the moment you choose clarity over comfort — again and again."

This form of leadership also requires a certain emotional discipline. You have learned, through experience, that not every request deserves urgency and not every decision benefits from speed. You refuse to be pulled into cycles of panic that others create from their own lack of preparation. Instead, you ground yourself in the long view. You take the time to think, even when the room is rushing. You ask questions that others overlook. You offer rationale where shortcuts would be easier. This steadiness is not resistance—it is responsibility. It is the quiet promise you make to the work itself.

There is also a particular strength in how you communicate. You do not use your voice to dominate the room; you use it to clarify the path forward. When you speak, you do so with intention, offering context that helps others see the landscape more fully. When you push back, you do so with reasoning, not rebellion. When you decline a direction, you offer alternatives grounded in understanding rather than ego. People may not always agree with you in the moment, but they recognize, in time, that your clarity protects the integrity of the work.

Becoming the leader your workplace deserves also means refusing to adopt the habits of those who frustrate you. You choose not to recreate their cycles of urgency or their reliance on reaction. You choose not to ignore information or allow confusion to grow in silence. You choose structure over chaos, preparation over scrambling, and vision over convenience. These choices are not always easy, especially in environments where short-sightedness is normalized, but you make them because you understand their long-term impact.

As your leadership deepens, something begins to shift within the people around you. They start showing up differently—not because you demanded it, but because your steadiness invites their best work. They trust your judgment because you've proven that your decisions are grounded in understanding. They ask for your perspective because they know you will see what they missed. They follow your lead not out of obligation, but because your clarity brings direction to places where they once felt lost. Your presence changes the emotional temperature of the room.

There is a quiet realization that follows: leadership is less about directing others and more about elevating the environment. You become the leader your workplace deserves by creating the conditions that allow everyone—yourself included—to rise. You do not wait for perfect circumstances or a perfectly constructed hierarchy. You lead because the work needs someone who sees the larger picture, someone who can hold both vision and responsibility, someone who understands that progress doesn't happen accidentally. You lead because you know how.

By the time this understanding fully takes root, the gap between who you were and who you are becoming feels almost seamless. You no longer question whether your instincts are valid. You no longer second-guess your clarity. You no longer wonder whether you are meant to lead. The answer reveals itself in the consistency of your actions, in the steadiness of your decisions, and in the way others naturally look to you when direction is needed.

Leadership is no longer a role waiting for approval—it is the truth you've been walking toward your entire career.

> "Being the visionary in the room is both a burden and a calling — but it is never a mistake."

CHAPTER 11

When You're the Visionary in the Room

"Integrity is doing the right thing, even when no one is watching."

— C. S. Lewis

There is a specific kind of isolation that comes from being the person who sees farther than the leadership around you. It doesn't announce itself loudly; it settles over time, in the small moments where you recognize that your instincts, your clarity, your pace, and your expectations sit in a completely different universe than the environment you are asked to work within. You hear the question being asked, and you already know the question that should have been asked. You watch the team scramble to recreate documents, and you already know which folder holds the version that would answer everything. You see the misunderstanding forming before the words are even spoken. It's a strange experience—knowing you're not just ahead, but often alone in that forward space.

At first, this separation doesn't feel like isolation. It feels like competence. You carry a sense of readiness that others rarely match. You connect information without effort, anticipate issues before they take shape, and navigate tasks with an understanding that seems to come from a deeper place than the assignment itself. People turn to you because they trust your reasoning. They rely on you because you bring order to confusion. They lean on your judgment because it consistently proves reliable. For a while, this feels like purpose.

The difficulty comes when your clarity begins colliding with leadership that cannot comprehend what you see. You try explaining the broader implications, but your insight is dismissed as unnecessary detail. You raise concerns early, only to watch them unfold months later exactly as you predicted. You offer direction, but the leader is too overwhelmed to recognize that you've handed them the solution they've been searching for. Over time, you realize that the gap between what you know and what they can hold is not temporary—it is structural.

This gap does something subtle to your spirit. You find yourself speaking more carefully, choosing moments with precision, because you know that your clarity can make others uncomfortable. Vision has a way of exposing what short-sighted leadership would prefer to ignore. When you point toward the future, they hear criticism of the present. When you highlight risks, they interpret it as resistance. When you decline a direction because you understand its consequences, they take it as defiance rather than protection. You are not challenging their authority—you are challenging the limits of their thinking. The misunderstanding becomes its own burden.

Yet even in that tension, there is a deeper truth: your perspective is not a disruption; it is an asset. The discomfort it creates is not a flaw in you—it is a limitation in them. Visionaries do not unsettle environments because they intend to; they unsettle environments because they reveal what could exist beyond the edges of habit and fear. This revelation changes the emotional climate of a room, even when no one acknowledges the source. You feel the weight of that shift, even when others do not.

The hardest part is the sense of responsibility that follows. You know the consequences of the wrong decision long before the decision is made. You know which direction brings stability and which direction brings confusion. You know which path strengthens the work and which path breaks it. That knowledge carries pressure, not because you doubt your judgment, but because you understand the cost of silence. You become the person who must speak when others hesitate, who must clarify when others remain unsure, who must steady the group when leadership falters. Your presence becomes a safeguard even when the title does not reflect it.

There is also a quiet grief that forms beneath the surface. You grieve the time wasted on rework that could have been avoided. You grieve the effort spent navigating confusion that never needed to exist. You grieve the opportunities missed because someone refused to lift their eyes and see what was possible. The grief doesn't come from ego; it comes from wanting better for the work, for the team, for the mission you care about. When you are the visionary in the room, you carry the weight of what could be—not because you were asked to, but because you cannot help but see it.

Yet within this grief lies a profound strength. You develop patience rooted not in resignation, but in wisdom. You learn when to step forward and when to step aside. You learn which battles require your voice and which ones will resolve themselves in time. You learn how to lead even when the organization has not named you as such. Visionaries often lead from the margins before they ever lead from the center. Their influence is felt long before it is acknowledged.

"When you're the visionary, your strength is misunderstood until the moment the team finally needs the clarity only you could see."

What surprises you most is how many people quietly depend on your steadiness. They may never say it directly, but they gravitate toward your energy. They mirror your clarity because it feels safe. They follow your suggestions because they recognize truth in them, even when they cannot articulate why. You become the anchor they lean on during uncertainty, the person who holds the work together when leadership cannot. Without intending to, you become the standard others measure themselves against.

In time, a deeper understanding forms—one that softens the frustration and reveals the meaning beneath your role. Being the visionary in the room is not a punishment; it is a calling. You were not meant to fit into systems built on short-sightedness. You were meant to elevate them. You were not meant to follow leaders who cannot see past today. You were meant to become the leader who understands tomorrow. Every moment of tension, every instance where you felt unseen or unheard, has only honed your ability to lead with intention, clarity, and courage.

By the time this truth settles, the isolation begins to feel different. What once felt like distance now feels like distinction. You stop apologizing for your insight. You stop shrinking your perspective to match what the room can hold. You stop feeling responsible for others' limitations. You recognize that the very qualities that once made you feel out of place are the qualities that define your leadership.

You are the visionary not because the room needed one, but because you were born one. And once you accept that, the way you walk through every space changes.

"Revolutions don't always begin with noise — sometimes they begin with someone quietly seeing farther than the rest."

CHAPTER 12

The Quiet Revolution of Forward Thinking

"The future belongs to those who believe in the beauty of their dreams."

— *Eleanor Roosevelt*

There comes a moment when you understand that forward thinking is not simply a professional skill; it is a way of moving through the world. It shapes how you make decisions, how you interpret challenges, and how you understand your responsibility to the work entrusted to you. For a long time, you may have seen it as something ordinary—a habit, an instinct, a quiet ability to connect information. But once you witness the contrast between environments guided by vision and those consumed by reaction, you realize that forward thinking is nothing short of revolutionary.

The revolution begins subtly. It starts with a decision to slow down where others rush, to understand where others scramble, to seek meaning where others settle for motion. You begin to recognize that clarity is not accidental; it is crafted with intention. Direction is not inherited; it is built through thoughtful choices. Momentum is not created by urgency; it is created by alignment. These truths reshape how you approach the work. You stop measuring productivity by how much is done in a day and start measuring it by how much remains stable tomorrow.

This shift extends beyond your own responsibilities. People notice when someone consistently thinks ahead. They see the steadiness in your decisions, the purpose in your questions, the way you refuse to be pulled into unnecessary chaos. Without announcing it, you change the tempo of the room. Meetings feel calmer because you bring context others haven't considered. Projects feel grounded because you anticipate the steps that would otherwise be overlooked. The work feels intentional because you refuse to settle for anything less.

As you continue to lead with this mindset, something else becomes clear: forward thinking is generous. It lifts people, not just projects. It creates room for others to contribute without fear of misalignment. When you share context, others feel empowered. When you articulate the bigger picture, others begin to see their place in it. When you design systems that prevent confusion, you give people the space to perform at their highest level. Your clarity becomes a form of compassion—a way of reducing unnecessary burden on those who simply want to do good work.

This generosity becomes even more evident when you observe how the work evolves. Teams under forward-thinking leadership experience fewer crises, fewer late-night scrambles, fewer moments of panic engineered by poor planning. The emotional landscape shifts from tension to trust. People take initiative because they understand the direction. They innovate because they feel safe. They speak up because the environment supports their voice rather than silencing it. Forward thinking creates a culture of calm competence, something rare and deeply valued.

Still, the revolution is not always easy. Forward thinkers often navigate environments resistant to change, surrounded by people who feel threatened by clarity or overwhelmed by the idea of long-term responsibility. It can feel lonely to hold a vision others do not yet recognize. But even in those moments, the power of your mindset remains unchanged. You continue seeing what is possible. You continue preparing for what others ignore. You continue advocating for systems that elevate rather than exhaust. The resistance may slow the pace, but it does not diminish the path.

> **"Forward thinking is not a strategy — it is a quiet revolution inside the people brave enough to imagine something better."**

With time, the impact of your approach becomes impossible to deny. The projects you touch carry a different kind of stability. The conversations you lead produce a different level of insight. The teams you influence develop a different caliber of confidence. Forward thinking doesn't just change outcomes—it changes people. It teaches them to pause, to consider, to understand before reacting. It invites them to rise to a standard they had forgotten they were capable of meeting.

Eventually, the revolution becomes personal. You begin to grasp what your leadership means beyond the workplace. You understand that you are not simply trying to create smoother workflows—you are shaping environments where people feel safe, respected, and capable. Your vision becomes a form of care. Your structure becomes a form of protection. Your clarity becomes a form of hope. This understanding transforms how you see yourself. You stop viewing your instinct for foresight as a burden in spaces that cannot match it, and instead recognize it as a calling.

The truth is simple but profound: forward thinkers do not wait for the world to change before they decide to lead. They lead in the world as it is, knowing that their presence alone can shift its direction. They carry a kind of quiet power—steady, thoughtful, grounded. It does not shout for attention, yet it shapes everything around it. You have been walking in this power for years, often without recognition, often without support, but always with intention. Now, you see it clearly.

And once that clarity settles, the revolution no longer feels quiet at all. It feels like purpose. It feels like alignment. It feels like the beginning of everything you were meant to build.

"The future always rewards the ones who prepared for it while everyone else was focused on surviving today."

CONCLUSION

The Future Belongs to the Visionaries

"The best way to predict the future is to create it."

— *Peter Drucker*

There comes a moment in every forward-thinking professional's journey when the noise around them finally fades, and a difficult truth becomes clear: the limits placed on their ideas were never their own. For a long time, it's easy to mistake confusion above you for a sign that your thinking is misplaced. When leadership cannot grasp what you see, you may wonder whether your ideas are premature, impractical, or simply unwelcome. But over time, the pattern reveals itself. The hesitation was never yours. It belonged to leaders constrained by fear, narrow frames, or an inability to look beyond the present moment.

That realization changes how you carry yourself. It loosens the quiet grip of self-doubt that forms when your clarity moves faster than the room. It frees you from shrinking your thinking so others can remain comfortable. It breaks the habit of second-guessing insight simply because it isn't immediately understood. Once you recognize that your vision was not the problem, you stop apologizing for it. You stop dimming it. You stop packaging it to fit inside someone else's limits. The fog clears, and what remains is a grounded understanding of who you are and how you lead.

Many organizations are built to preserve momentum, not direction. They resist change not because innovation is flawed, but because vision disrupts routines that feel safe. Clarity unsettles those who rely on urgency to maintain control. Long-term thinking challenges leaders who have only learned how to react. In these environments, forward thinkers often feel out of place—not because they lack discipline or focus, but because their perspective exposes what others have never been asked to consider. Still, they continue to notice patterns, name risks, and advocate for direction, even when the culture rewards motion over meaning.

At some point, a shift occurs. Forward-thinking professionals stop waiting for recognition and begin standing fully in their competence. They trust their reasoning enough to speak with conviction. They share ideas without shrinking them. They let the quality of their work carry weight where words once fell flat. This shift isn't about proving superiority or seeking validation. It's about alignment—between how you think, how you work, and how you lead.

When that alignment settles in, leadership becomes steadier. You no longer expend energy trying to be understood by people unwilling or unable to think beyond the immediate moment. Instead, you invest in building, refining, and designing systems that last. Your focus shifts from survival to intention. From reacting to shaping. From managing today's problems to preparing for what comes next.

This is the transformation at the heart of this book.

It holds space for the frustration of working under short-sighted leadership, the exhaustion of repeated rework, and the quiet isolation of seeing the path before anyone else does. But it also points to what emerges from that experience: discernment, confidence, and a deeper understanding of what leadership truly requires. Each chapter has returned to the same truth—visionary thinking is not disruptive. It is essential.

By now, the distinction is clear. Leadership is not authority. Activity is not progress. Urgency is not strategy. Real leadership anticipates. It designs. It accounts for what comes after the decision, not just what comes before the deadline. It builds systems instead of cycles and creates space for people to do meaningful work without constantly bracing for the next fire.

If this book has done its work, you no longer question whether your instinct to think ahead is valid. You understand the value of foresight, the discipline of preparation, and the responsibility that comes with seeing beyond the moment. You recognize that clarity is not arrogance, and that forward thinking is not impatience—it is leadership.

The future does not belong to the loudest voice in the room or the busiest calendar on the screen. It belongs to those willing to look past today, to imagine what could exist tomorrow, and to build toward it with intention.

And once you see that, you move forward differently—rooted, deliberate, and no longer waiting for permission to lead.

Reflection Questions

These questions are designed to help you slow down, look inward, and name the truths that surfaced as you moved through each chapter. Take your time with them; clarity deepens when you pause long enough to understand what the experience revealed about you. There are no right answers here—only honest ones, and those are the ones that change everything.

1. Myth of Busy Leadership

Where in your work or life have you mistaken motion for progress, and what helped you finally see the difference?

2. The Leader Who Can't See Past Today

What patterns of short-sighted leadership have you witnessed, and how have those patterns shaped the way you now view authority?

3. The Cost of Reaction-Based Leadership

How has reactive leadership cost you time, energy, creativity, or morale — and what insight did those moments give you about what real leadership requires?

4. The Bottleneck Effect

Think of a time when leadership became the bottleneck. What opportunities died quietly because one person couldn't make a timely or strategic decision?

5. The Psychology Behind Short-Sighted Leaders

What fears or insecurities do you now recognize beneath the surface of short-sighted leaders, and how has that understanding changed your emotional response to them?

6. Visionary Leadership: What It Actually Looks Like

Which qualities of visionary leadership come naturally to you — and which ones are inviting you to grow?

7. Leaders Who Build Systems Instead of Cycles

Where do you see cycles repeating in your organization or personal life, and what system—simple or complex—could break that repetition?

8. The Second-Order Consequence Mindset

What second- or third-order consequences have you noticed that others seemed to miss, and how did seeing farther alter the way you approached the situation?

9. Experiencing Different Leader Types

How has working under both visionary and short-sighted leaders shaped your own expectations for leadership and workplace culture?

10. Becoming the Leader Your Workplace Deserves

What practical steps are you ready to take to become a more intentional, strategic, and future-focused leader?

11. When You're the Visionary in the Room

When have you realized you were the visionary in the room, and how did that awareness change the way you showed up?

---

12. The Quiet Revolution of Forward Thinking

In what ways are you already participating in the quiet revolution of forward thinking — and where might your next horizon be calling you?

Take your time. Answer honestly. Your responses are the blueprint for your next level.

Notes

Notes

Notes

Notes

Notes

Notes

www.ingramcontent.com/pod-product-compliance
Lightning Source LLC
Chambersburg PA
CBHW071411160426
42813CB00085B/1057